WOMEN OF COUNTRY

The Life, Times, & Music™ Series

WOMEN OF COUNTRY

The Life, Times, & Music™ Series

Andrew G. Hager

Friedman/Fairfax
Publishers

Acknowledgments

Special thanks to Nick Shaffran, whose knowledge and
passion for the music of the women of country clarified the direction
of this book, and to Nathaniel Marunas, editor extraordinaire,
for his patience, philanthropy, and unflinching ability to make
writers like me look good.

A FRIEDMAN GROUP BOOK

Copyright © 1994 by Michael Friedman Publishing Group, Inc.

All rights reserved. No part of this publication may be reproduced,
stored in a retrieval system, or transmitted, in any form or by any means,
electronic, mechanical, photocopying, recording, or otherwise,
without the prior written permission of the publisher.

ISBN 1-56799-085-1

THE LIFE, TIMES, & MUSIC^{TM} SERIES: WOMEN OF COUNTRY
was prepared and produced by
Michael Friedman Publishing Group, Inc.
15 West 26th Street
New York, New York, 10010

Editor: Nathaniel Marunas
Art Director: Jeff Batzli
Designer: Lynne Yeamans
Photography Editor: Jennifer Crowe McMichael
Compilation Producer: Nick Shaffran

Cover Photography Credits Horseshoe: ©Martin Rogers/FPG International; Hat &
Boots: ©Laurance B. Aiuppy/FPG International; Dolly Parton: ©Nancy Barr/Retna
Ltd.; Patsy Montana: Frank Driggs Collection.

Grateful acknowledgment is given to authors, publishers, and photographers for permission to reprint material. Every effort has been made to determine copyright owners of photographs and illustrations. In the case of any omissions, the publishers will
be pleased to make suitable acknowledgments in future editions.

Printed in the United States of America

For bulk purchases and special sales, please contact:
Friedman/Fairfax Publishers
15 West 26th Street
New York, NY 10010
(212) 685-6610 FAX (212) 685-1307

Contents

Introduction

Country music is a living example of the creative power of the heart; it is an art of community inclusion that is founded on the bedrock of structural simplicity and the expression of bold personal messages. Country music is evidence that if performers are true to themselves and their experiences they can reach the hearts of millions. Throughout the quickly changing twentieth century, country music has worked to bind us to our past, to help us survive present circumstances, and to build dreams toward the future. It seems obvious that female country musicians feel as strongly as men about their

The women of country music have been playing a significant role in the struggle for sexual equality since the early days of recording and radio. Today, country's female songwriters continue to fuel the women's liberation movement.

heritage and their circumstances, but throughout the history of commercial music the contributions of these women have been trivialized. Through four generations of struggle in the musical workplace, women have fought the preconceptions of a male-dominated society, pushing incrementally toward equal treatment.

Left: Following the Civil War, southern wives and mothers maintained both the home and farm while their husbands and sons went to work in early rural industries, such as phosphate pits and lumber camps.

In country music in particular women have had to fight prejudice—about everything from their ability to travel alone to whether there was a market at all for their music. Most importantly, they have fought the presumption that an expanded role for women in society would be the demise of the "nuclear" family. Through a seemingly neverending battle, these women, who were and are true country musicians, have overcome the cultural biases that have kept them from their life path.

The story of country music is inextricably linked to the unique history of the American South, which has posed very specific problems for women both inside and outside of country music. Southern white

Below: As the slaves fled the South in the wake of the Civil War, the labor force changed, drastically affecting the lives of families across North America.

tenant farmers in the mid- to late nineteenth century, for example, became powerless, politically and economically, as the average family income dropped and the availability of work dwindled because of the changes in a labor force swelled by the emancipation of the slaves. The marks of civility and gentility that had once defined white southern culture were forever out of grasp for the working southern white. One great symbol that separated the rich white from the poor white was the duties, or lack thereof, of the women. During

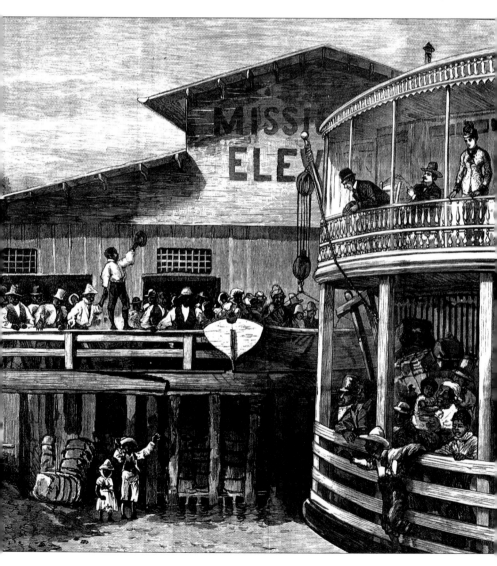

Reconstruction, many wives of the white tenant-farming households "shamefully" had to maintain the home and farm by themselves while their husbands and sons took to the cities looking for more work after the season's crops had been brought in. (The problems of women have not been limited to the American South, however. North American society in general has been slow to show any respect for the abilities of women outside the domestic sphere, and little respect for southerners in general.)

It is encouraging that within a single century, women of both the North and the South have struggled from a second-class role to increasingly powerful positions in government and industry. It is some evidence that, as with the success and popularity of the determined women of country music, the scales of justice inevitably tilt in favor of those who pursue a community-conscious cause. Their cause has not been one of revolution, intended to abolish the family or society, but rather an evolution toward inclusion and participation for all women. Female singers, songwriters, and instrumentalists have carved out their place in history, insuring a path for those who follow while allowing the daughters of their songs to move closer to achieving the goal of equality and empowerment in the male-dominated country music industry.

The Oral Tradition

Strangely enough, the written history of country music, despite the genre's deeply rooted traditions, is only as old as recorded sound. Before the radio and phonograph, the music of rural peoples had been preserved through an oral tradition of performances by locals. In the brief moments these people had for socializing between work

Jimmie Rodgers, known as both "the Blue Yodeler" and "Jimmie the Brakeman," was the first star of commercial country music.

and more work, their music defined their way of life. Fiddles, guitars, banjos, Dobros, dulcimers, and above all the human voice praised God, mourned lost love, and laughed out loud at the perils of rural living. The music was and is a rich blend of each contributor's ethnic background, varying greatly from one region of the South to another.

Professional musicians before the advent of radio were limited to only two real venues. The first was the opera house (soon to become the vaudeville circuit), where they performed as part of a collection of novelty acts, and theater and magic shows that came primarily from the North. The music performed in these venues, if not comedic, was predominantly European (the operetta was very popular at this time), serving the southern masses as a reminder of the "culture" the South had left behind.

The only other way for a southern musician to make a living before commercialized music was to travel with a medicine show. "Doctors," prescribing everything from opium for pregnant women to cocaine for the depressed to colored water for ailments of every possible description, understood that the way to the hearts of rural Americans was through the songs of southern musicians. The earliest history of country music is in fact made up mostly of musicians who earned their living entertaining on medicine shows. Jimmie "the Blue Yodeler" Rodgers (1897–1933), Ernest Tubb (1914–1984), Hank Williams (1923–1953), and many others began their careers by promoting drugs for these doctors.

Of the small number of these professional musicians traveling through the South, few were women, as a woman traveling alone would surely gain an unsavory reputation.

Industrialization and the Music

In its infancy, the northern-based phonograph industry defined the parameters of "American music." Tunes from the relatively recently conquered rebel states were not exactly considered American. Culture, as established by northern industrialists, was a product exported westward from the Northeast through the new frontier. Nasal, twangy singing by southerners seemed to northerners to be wholly unpromotable.

The birth of radio, however, began breaking down the barriers between the northern and southern United States. An intra-continental communication network began linking the vast North American continent, potentially ending the isolationist conceits of each region.

Women had their first taste of success with the advent of radio. "Barn Dance" programs featuring women performers made the commercial viability of women in country music apparent.

The Carter Family

The Carter Family has most likely had the largest influence on folk and country music of any American group. Nearly all folk musicians have admitted their debt to country music's first family. Each member of the Carter Family brought to their music not only the history of the tunes of early settlers but a glimpse of the music of the future as well. Their descendants have described the women of the original Carter Family as "the first truly liberated women," who were concerned solely with the quality and content of their music, ignoring outright the presumptions audience members would have about two women on the road away from home and children.

Alvin Pleasant Delaney Carter (1891–1960), a regular church quartet member and locally popular bass singer, had a passion for and a vast knowledge of traditional folk songs. When he was not working on the farm, A.P. (as he was called) spent his free time singing with family and friends or searching out new material among the inhabitants of the Clinch Mountain region of Virginia.

In 1915 he married Sara Dougherty (1898–1979) of Flat Woods, Virginia. A fine singer in her own right, Sara also played the autoharp. Her voice, sailing above music well grounded by A.P.'s bass voice, has been described as haunting, eerily angelic yet emotionally distant.

Sara's cousin Maybelle Addington (1909–1978) regularly visited the Carter household in Maces Springs and soon became a major contributor to the local music

The Carter women—particularly Maybelle (second from left) and her daughters June (left), Anita (second from right), and Helen (right)—are pivotal figures in the history of country music.

With the help of Johnny Cash (right), Maybelle Carter (left) and her daughters regained the national limelight during the 1960s through appearances on both radio and television.

the mountains of Virginia. Peer, upon hearing their music, quickly bought six of their songs. The family went back to Maces Springs ecstatic, unaware that this would not be the last they'd see of Mr. Ralph Peer.

Within a few months Peer had made another offer to record the family, this time in Camden, New Jersey. The strange and exciting trip up North resulted in the purchase and recording of the family's most popular songs. For seventy-five dollars per song, Peer and Victor Records became the proud owners of "Wildwood Flower" and "Keep on the Sunny Side." In those days, before litigation over artistic ownership, royalties from record sales were unheard of. The Carters were no exception to the rule.

Although Sara and A.P. separated in 1933, the family continued to tour and record until 1942, at which time Sara, again marrying into the family, wedded Coy Bayes, A.P.'s cousin.

Since that time there have been two attempts to form an all-new Carter Family. The first was with A.P. and Sara's two children, Joe and Janette, which quickly broke up due to lack of interest. The second and more successful group was composed of the Carter family women, Maybelle, June, Anita, and Helen. Appearing regularly with June's new love, Johnny Cash (1932–), the Carter women regained national attention and brought full circle the history of twentieth-century southern music.

community with her unique style of guitar playing, soon to be termed the "Carter scratch." Plucking a bass line with her thumb and carrying the melody with the other fingers, Maybelle, probably without knowing it, had changed the way in which the guitar was to be played by folk musicians forever. She, too, was soon a Carter, marrying A.P.'s brother Ezra.

The first family of country music began their rise to national attention in August of 1927 with the help of legendary talent scout Ralph Peer. Hearing of a search for local talent by a northern phonograph entrepreneur, A.P., Sara, and Maybelle drove the thirty miles from their house in Maces Springs to Bristol, Virginia. It was not only the search for recognition that brought them to Bristol but the advertised price of fifty dollars per song, an amount unheard of in

A search for wider economic markets, fueled by this new rivalry between radio and phonography, led to the reconsideration of the "rural" population. The radio, at first a fad, was soon to be considered a necessity in every American home. It is estimated that by 1929 every third home had a radio. This is astounding considering that the radio industry was at the time only nine years old.

The first recorded country musician, harmonica player Deford Bailey, was one of the original members of the Grand Ole Opry.

The first country star born out of this commercialization was Jimmie Rodgers, a veteran brakeman and waterboy for the Ohio and Mobile railroad lines who serviced the tracks from one major southern city to the next. Working side by side with first- and second-generation freedmen, Jimmie became familiar with the musical language of the African-American. It is this influence that made Jimmie Rodgers an overnight sensation when he turned to music as a profession (after tuberculosis caused his early retirement from the railroad). The blending of culturally diverse music in a southern society coming to terms with a reconstructed South resonated strongly in the twenties with whites who, for the first time in American history, worked hand in hand with former slaves. Jimmie Rodgers, the father of country music, may have been the first white man to sing the blues. With the help of talent scout Ralph Peer and propelled by the headspinning growth of commercial music, Jimmie Rodgers became the first household name in country music.

The first recorded country musician, though his popularity did not immortalize him, was Deford Bailey, an African-American harmonica player. When the Grand Ole Opry was established, Bailey also became one of the original members of that prestigious Nashville company. Just as interestingly, he was the first Opry regular to be fired under questionable circumstances. (Not until the late fifties would there be another successful African-American country performer, Charlie Pride. Pride broke ground by becoming one of only ten music performers in any field to have ten albums make it to the top ten in record sales.)

Charlie Pride is one of the most successful country musicians of all time, having had ten of his albums reach the top ten on the Billboard charts.

The phonograph, nearly squelched in the battle against the radio by 1923, survived the drought in sales. Until 1927 and the discovery and recording of the Carter Family, with Maybelle Carter on guitar, the phonograph business recorded only men, which left the music field wide open for another radio victory.

The Barn Dances

Atlanta's WSB, the first high-powered southern radio station, heralded the beginning of a new age in American music. The enthusiastic audience response to WSB's time-filling local talent show began shaping rural music as a commodity. One radio station after another, popping up here and there throughout the United States, began bringing what was by then termed "hillbilly music" to their listeners in the "barn dance" format.

In 1922, radio took a chance and brought a woman to the forefront of the music as a solo star. Contralto Grace Wilson (1890–1962), a vaudeville and musical-comedy singing star, made her radio

Grace Wilson, a thirty-six-year veteran of the National Barn Dance, was known as the "Girl with a Million Friends."

Sunshine Sue (center), aka Sue Workman, was originally a member of the all-female band The Happy Valley Girls. Another original member, fiddler Ramona Riggins (left), rose to fame with her husband and duet partner, Grandpa Jones.

debut on WTAS out of Elgin, Illinois, introducing the songs "I'd Love to Live in Loveland with You," "In the Shade of the Old Apple Tree," and most memorably, "Bringing Home the Bacon." Her career as a star of the barn dance radio circuit was the longest of any performer, spanning over thirty-six years.

Needless to say, Grace Wilson opened the minds of radio entrepreneurs to the idea of women stars. A veritable glut of talented women singers and musicians began making headway in radio. Firecracker Cousin Emmy out of WSB in Atlanta played the dots off the five-string banjo; Sunshine Sue shone at the *Ole Dominion Barn*

Each member of The Coon Creek Girls was named for a flower. Their theme song, "Flowers Blooming in the Wild Wood," was wildly popular with their audiences.

Dance; The Coon Creek Girls played on Kentucky's *Renfro Valley Barn Dance*; guitarist Lulu Belle performed on Chicago's WLS; and Minnie Pearl (1913–), forever immortalized on Nashville's Grand Ole Opry stage, all quickly became celebrities.

Because the pay for radio performance was next to nothing (one dollar per act at the Grand Ole Opry), traveling from town to town at night after the radio show became a financial necessity. The townspeople of rural America were less receptive to women singers outside of their radio performances, however, and gave them second billing

Part of the duo Lulu Belle and Scotty, Lulu Belle (on guitar), aka Myrtle Eleanor Cooper, was the successful daughter of a convicted moonshiner.

to the male performers. The myth of the wanton woman on the road also persisted, making it imperative for successful bands to be family (or at least to pretend to be related).

Western Swing

The western swing style, a hybrid of Mexican mariachi music, the blues, Louisiana's Dixieland jazz, and, oddly enough, Hawaiian guitar,

Patsy Montana (1912–)

Hot Springs, Arkansas, native Patsy Montana became lead singer for The Prairie Ramblers sometime during their fifteen-year stint on the *National Barn Dance*. Montana's first and only major hit, "I Wanna Be a Cowboy's Sweetheart," sold more than a million copies.

began developing in the twenties, finally becoming a national obsession by the mid-thirties. Women involved in this musical transformation took a back seat to their male counterparts but contributed, albeit minimally, to its growth and development.

The Dixieland influence on country music, it is believed, began as part of the Texas sound during the oil boom of the early twenties. At the time, Louisianians were rushing to the Lone Star State for a quick, messy profit as roughnecks; they brought with them the spicy Dixieland sound. The falsetto howls and the guitar ensemble work were not recent imports to the region, as were the Dixieland sound and the Hawaiian guitar, but were remnants of Spain and Mexico's days of ownership of *Tejas*.

The origin of the Hawaiian sound in western swing and country music in general goes back to a World War I stage show in the boomtown of Kusa, Oklahoma, in 1917. Walter Kolomoku and his

Bob Dunn, pictured here with the Panhandle Cowboys and Indians (of Oklahoma), is responsible for the introduction of Hawaiian slide guitar into country music.

Hawaiian group were approached after their concert by an excited listener, guitarist Bob Dunn, who wanted to learn how to play their homespun style of twangy steel guitar. Through correspondence with Kolomoku, Dunn became a gifted player and went so far as to amplify his instrument. By 1927 Dunn joined the Oklahoma-based group the Panhandle Cowboys and Indians, a progenitor of the western swing sound. Although Dunn, who was shot to death in Dallas in 1931, did not ride the wave of western swing to its eventual glory, the electrified steel guitar that he introduced remains a fixture in country music.

The most popular western country swing performer, Bob Wills (1905–1975), began his career as a fiddler with friend and guitarist Herman Arnspiger, playing house parties around the Fort Worth area. After a stint at WBAP, Wills, Arnspiger, and vocalist Milton Brown landed a job with KFLZ promoting Light Crust Flour.

Rose Maddox (1925–   )

Taking second billing to the band she was lead singer for, Rose Maddox helped bring her family to the forefront of country music. The Maddox Brothers and Sister Rose quickly grasped national attention, billed as "The Most Colorful Hillbilly Band in All the Land."

In 1933, the Maddox clan left their home in Alabama, migrating as part of the Okie Rush to San Joaquin, California. Holding on to the memories of their Alabama home through song, brothers Cal, Henry, Fred, and Don played the guitar, harmonica, mandolin, and double bass, respectively, while the pure church-choir voice of Rose soared above their rhythmic sound. The family took to wearing loud costumes and depended on brother Cal to tell jokes to warm up their growing audiences.

Before two of the brothers were drafted for service during World War II, the family played regularly in Modesto, California, on KTRB, and at night traveled from rodeos and honky tonks to piece together a living. After the brothers' army tours were over, the band began a ten-year recording career with Columbia, Decca, and the notorious 4 Star recording companies. Their greatest single success came with the recording of Woody Guthrie's "Philadelphia Lawyer." In 1949 they claimed their second national success with the rowdy "Mamma Says It's Naughty," and in 1952 had another major hit with "Old Black Choo Choo."

With the help of KWKH's *Louisiana Hayride*, The Maddox Brothers and Sister Rose continued to capture the hearts of Americans until they broke up in 1956.

Rose pursued a solo career during the sixties, producing many hit songs including "Gambler's Love," "Sing a Little Song of Heartache," and "Down to the River," each recorded with Capitol Records. She also sang with Bill Monroe (1911–   ), Red Smiley (1925–1972), and Donna Stoneman (1947–   ) of The Stoneman Family Revival.

In the seventies Rose Maddox decided to retrace the path she had taken, back to her roots in country music, recording with specialist labels Takoma and Arhoolie.

The Maddox siblings grew up on a Farm Services Administration camp during the Great Depression.

Bob Wills, seen here with several members of the Texas Playboys, toured the country by bus for over a decade. It is said that Bob never fired anyone from his band—he just stopped driving by their house to pick them up for the gigs.

Their duties, unfortunately, were not exclusively related to the performance of music and the promotion of their sponsor's product, but included loading and unloading flour at the Light Crust warehouse and driving deliveries to Fort Worth–area stores. The Light Crust Doughboys finally landed a two-song deal with Victor Records after the inclusion of "Sleepy" Johnson on guitar and banjo. Wills left the Light Crust Doughboys following another of many contract disputes with their sponsor, and soon after that formed what would become the most highly regarded western swing band in the country, Bob Wills and the Texas Playboys. By 1938 their number had increased to fourteen members, four of whom were vocalists. Their popular female singer, Evelyn McKinney, was the wife of Wills' second vocalist, Dean McKinney.

In 1933 a Kentucky swing band, The Prairie Ramblers, added their first female singer, yodeler Patsy Montana. Her single, "I Wanna Be a Cowboy's Sweetheart," was the first song recorded by a woman to sell more than a million copies. Patsy broke ground for women by being the first to travel with men who were not related to her and demanding equal pay for her work. "They wanted to pay me less 'cause I was a girl but I stood my ground," explains Patsy. "I wudn't scared. . . I just stood my ground."

The Singing Cowboy and His Gal

As the United States became consumed with the myth of the Wild West, the image of the hillbilly as the charming southern fool began to be replaced by the image of a newer, more respectable, overdressed western cowboy. Demand for songs from the new frontier

Gene Autry's first record, "That Silver Haired Daddy Of Mine," sold over five million copies.

mounted quickly in the East and, understandably, country songwriters in the South supplied the rest of the country with the sounds of the prairies, abandoning the heritage of their own regions.

The first western star, Gene Autry (1907–), was a radio and recording star from Oklahoma. As legend has it, Will Rogers (1879–1935) himself, hearing Autry play while visiting Oklahoma, told Gene to head to New York and become a singer. Thanks to the Great

Left: After his success on the silver screen, Tex Ritter became president of the Country Music Association. Below: Dale Evans, seen here with her second husband, Roy Rogers, married her first husband at fourteen and gave birth to a son the following year.

Depression and widespread unemployment, Autry had time to follow his dream.

By 1934, after several successful recordings and continued success in radio, Autry moved to California, quickly becoming "America's number one singing cowboy" of the movies. Although preceded by Ken Maynard as the first cowboy to sing on film, Autry to this day is considered the father of the western cowboys.

How the singing cowboys punched cows while dressed in pretty frilly outfits and yodeling one will never know, but the image was consumed wholeheartedly, making millionaires of Gene Autry, Tex Ritter (1905–1974), and Roy Rogers (1912–).

Cindy Walker

Cindy Walker was the first "music video" artist, having been recorded on film singing her drinking song "Seven Beers with the Wrong Man."

western film industry. All the songs in the eight films of Bob Wills were penned by Walker.

Her knack for meeting the musical needs of artists who were to cover the material made her skills invaluable. Eddy Arnold (1918–) covered her traditionally flavored song "Take Me in Your Arms and Hold Me" in 1950 as well as country pop numbers such as "You Don't Know Me." Artists such as Ernest Tubb ("Warm Red Wine"), Jim Reeves ("This Is It," 1965, and "Distant Drums,"

The daughter of a Texas cotton buyer, Cindy Walker became one of the most successful songwriters in country music history. On vacation with her father in Hollywood, Cindy had the great honor of meeting fellow Texan and father of western swing Bob Wills. Impressed with the young Walker's songwriting skills, Wills and the Texas Playboys recorded four of her songs on the Okeh label in July of 1941.

This happenstance relationship with Wills, one of the most influential male stars of country music, led to commercially lucrative deals writing music for the thriving

1966), and Hank Snow ("The Gold Rush Is Over," 1952) have Cindy Walker to thank for much of their commercial success.

With a career that spanned thirty years, Walker demonstrated an impressive ability to change with the ever-expanding definition of country. Writing everything from motion picture cowboy songs to rockabilly and bluegrass—even drinking songs—Walker continued to write hits all the way through the sixties. Cindy Walker was elected to the Songwriter's Hall of Fame of the Nashville Songwriters Association in 1970.

The women of the movies were peripherally important to the cowboy image, fulfilling the role of the singing girlfriend. What real cowboy could be contentedly single for an entire movie? The beautiful and talented Dale Evans (1912–), for instance, took a back seat to her husband Roy Rogers for over twenty pictures.

Outside the motion picture industry, the music of women singers began to be tested as a viable commercial product extensively during and directly following the World War II era. The radio and recording industry saw the rise of such female talent as Rosalie Allen (1924–), Jenny Lou Carson (1915–1978), Cousin Emmy (also earlier a barn dance star), and Molly O'Day (1923–1987). The women

Cousin Emmy, born Cynthia May Carver near Lamb, Kentucky, confessed that as a child she sang and entertained her cousins to keep from having to pick tobacco.

Guitarist, banjo player, and singer Molly O'Day has been called the female Hank Williams because of her honky-tonk singing style.

who made their way into business during this period were given the opportunity mostly because the men were abroad fighting the war. Once the men had returned home, the women country stars' impact, was de-emphasized. Despite their popularity, they were considered more of a halftime phenomenon than actual participants in the game; indeed, women singers would not be considered important to the direction of country music for two more decades.

The most substantial impact females of this era had was in songwriting. The eminently talented Cindy Walker composed songs for almost every singing cowboy. She also transcended the era itself to become one of the most successful female songwriters ever.

Through the thirties and forties the western was to continue to be the rage as one cowboy after another stepped onto the set and tested his credibility with the American audience. Bob Wills (of the Texas Playboys), Ernest Tubb, and many others had their turn in front of the movie camera.

Honky Tonk

Although women played a small role in the rough-and-tumble lifestyle of the honky tonk, it is important to mention the changes country music went through during the era directly following Prohibition. If it were not for the changes in sound and energy of the music during this time, the women who followed into rockabilly and the Nashville sound would have led distinctly different lives, both musically and personally.

The Texas oil boom of the twenties had a profound effect on the music of southern people. The roughnecks and drillers, who came from all over the South, brought with them a host of new musical ideas. This new music, combined with the furnacelike conditions of the industry's dangerous workplace and the clashing of cultures, made nightlife in the boomtowns of the South both lively and lawless. After the workday ended, satisfying the emotional needs of people who lived on the edge during working hours became more important than maintaining the usual standards of civility.

"Blood buckets," as the honky tonks came to be called, were loud saloons usually built on the outskirts of town so as to allow customers from both "dry" and "wet" counties to be within driving distance. Their location also served to keep the police at a distance and taxation to a minimum.

Kitty Wells (1919–)

Although preceded in popular record sales by Patsy Montana, Kitty Wells, whose voice is best described as sweet and simple, is considered the first female country star and the Queen of Country Music. Born Muriel Deason on August 30, 1919, in Nashville, Tennessee, Wells began her music career in gospel, singing with her sister as regulars on her hometown radio station WSIX.

In 1937 Muriel was married to entertainer Johnny Wright (1914–), co-member of the music group The Johnny and Jack Team. Throughout the rest of the thirties and forties she toured nationally with her husband's group, appearing on several country radio music programs, most notably Shreveport's KWKH *Louisiana Hayride*. In 1943 Muriel Wright, at the suggestion of her husband, changed her name to the showier Kitty Wells (after the popular folk song "Sweet Kitty Wells").

She began her recording career with Decca records in 1952. Her first three hits were "answer songs," rebuttals to other popular songs. Her first hit, "It Wasn't God Who Made Honky Tonk Angels," was written in response to Hank Thompson's "Wild Side of Life." Thompson's song was about good men gone bad at the hands of indecent women. Wells pointed out in "Honky Tonk Angels" that women driven from decency weren't born with the mission of corrupting men, but most likely had been corrupted by rowdy cowboys. It is interesting to note that her response had as great an impact on the commercial market as Thompson's original song, both placing in the top ten. Although her song can be seen as an expression of women's equality to men, Kitty has always seen herself as a woman whose role in society was, for the best of all involved, that of a good wife and mother before that of a bread-winning country music legend.

From those first recording dates in 1952 to the early sixties, Wells appeared as a regular cast member on the Grand Ole Opry, and in 1959 she became the first woman to sign a lifetime recording contract with Decca Records (soon to be MCA). By 1963 MCA had recorded over 461 singles and forty-three albums by Kitty Wells.

Wells' songs always remained on the forefront socially by addressing touchy issues, such as divorce, and by creating opportunities for the women who were to follow in her footsteps.

The Grand Ole Opry did not allow Kitty Wells to sing her hit "It Wasn't God Who Made Honky Tonk Angels" because it was "too outspoken."

Musicians who found themselves earning a living from work in these bars performed for audiences who yelled, broke bottles, and displayed a general disinterest in anything outside of drinking alcohol and fighting. To keep the ear of the listener, the music played by the country musician had to change. Songs like "Keep on the Sunny Side" no longer seemed appropriate.

The last song by the legendary father of honky tonk, Hank Williams, that became a hit before his death at the age of twenty-nine was "I'll Never Make It Out of This World Alive."

Lyrically, the music changed forever. The year-end-harvest-and-church-on-Sunday mentality, traditional folk song fare, was now only a memory of a time gone by. Songs like "Driving Nails in My Coffin (Every Time I Drink a Bottle of Booze)" reflected the changing perspectives of rural

In 1954 Jean Shepard released the first female concept album, entitled **Songs of a Love Affair.**

Americans who found themselves caught up in the Industrial Age.

Instrumentation also had to change. Traditionalists, typified by the producers of the barn dance radio shows throughout the nation, tried their best to exclude electric bass and guitar from the country format. Yet performers took up these instruments out of necessity, in order to be heard above the din of the bars' patrons, and folklorists and the old guard took up arms over this issue only to inevitably lose.

These changes in lyrics and instrumentation are reflected in the music of honky tonk's greatest star, Hank Williams. The son of an incapacitated, shell-shocked World War I veteran, Hank spent most of his young life earning money singing in the streets to feed himself and his mother. After a brief stint in Texas playing wherever there was money to be made, Williams returned to his hometown of Mobile, Alabama, to work as a welder during World War II. Following the war he moved to Nashville, determined to make it big in the music he loved. His lyrics, as raw as his powerful persona, were about his disinterest in respectable living, about lost love, and most of all about men basically being dogs. His passion for testing the outer limits of existence, fueled by alcohol and prescription drugs, finally cost him his life at the age of twenty-nine at the height of his international career.

The women who did dare to work the honky tonk circuit— Jean Shepard (1933–), Rose Maddox, and Goldie Hill (1933–)—were to find their success not in this era but in the years to follow.

Rockabilly

With the massive appeal of Hank Williams, country music began making headway into the popular music field. Artists from both musical camps began balancing between forms, blending country sounds with popular instrumentation and song structures to appeal to a greater audience. Since popular music by nature is ever-changing, the sounds country grabbed on to and called its own were products of specific historical influences and the desires of music listeners throughout the United States.

Struggling during the Depression, the country as a whole had wondered if a mechanized society, where every family had a home, a car, a radio, and spending money for the magic of the movies, was too big and unwieldy a dream. With an entire nation hard at work during the years following the Depression, however, the American Dream was reinvigorated.

Brenda Lee (1944–)

Brenda Mae Tarpley, born December 11, 1944, began her career in music at the age of five, winning a local talent contest in her hometown of Lithonia, Georgia. By the age of seven, Brenda was appearing regularly on the radio program *Starmakers' Revue* and as a guest on *TV Ranch*, both in Atlanta.

Brenda saw her career take hold in 1956 when country legend Red Foley asked her to perform on his radio show, the *Ozark Jubilee*. Foley's manager, Dub Albritten, began booking appearances for Foley and Tarpley as a duet, and the two appeared on every hit television show of the time. Steve Allen, Ed Sullivan, Red Skelton, Bob Hope, and Danny Thomas introduced Brenda Lee to North America.

Signing with Decca Records in that same year, 1956, Lee had her first country hit, "One Step at a Time." At the age most children hit puberty, Brenda was the leading female singer of country music.

Songs like "Dynamite" in 1957, "Sweet Nothin's" in 1959, and "Rockin' Around the Christmas Tree" made Brenda Lee an "acceptable" female counterpart to Elvis in America. She was someone who, as most Americans at the time were convinced, was too young to mean anything by her shaking hips. Ballads such as "I'm Sorry" and "As Usual" led her back to standard country, insuring her permanent place in the history of the music she adored.

By 1969, forty-eight of her singles and fifteen of her albums had reached the popular charts.

In the late 1950s and early 1960s, she was one of the leading popular singers in the United States and Europe.

At the age of six, Brenda Lee won her first singing competition and a spot in the cast of TV Ranch, which broadcast out of Atlanta on WAGA.

Since Elvis Presley 's death in 1977, his estate has made 400 million dollars a year from the sale of records, books, and memorabilia about and by him.

The children of the fifties were born into this dream as it was being realized. A fully explored and developed nation with sprawling urban centers from coast to coast was a fact. The possibilities seemed endless to a generation born into an already industrialized nation. As a result, North American society became polarized between two (often opposing) cultures: the young and the old.

Young people's lives, and by extension their music, reflected that mechanized society. Rhythm was everything. The cities themselves were underscored by a constant beat. There was no controversy among the young over the necessity of having drums in popular music. Driving rhythm was perceived to be as vital to music as the heartbeat is to the body. Rock and roll defined the growing fracture between generations.

Described fairly accurately as white-performed rhythm and blues, rock and roll heralded a new consensus on reality among young people. The idea of revolution, a breaking away from the past to embrace a new and very different world, seemed inevitable to the young and wholly dangerous to the ideals of their parents.

Elvis Presley (1935–1977) was the first and greatest example of this movement. A farm boy raised on Pentecostal church hymns and country music, he strayed from tradition in his teenage years and began listening to what his mother termed, as all mothers soon would, "the Devil's music." The African-American rhythm and blues, as played by the likes of Big Bill Broonzy (1897–1958) and Arthur Crudup (1905–1974), both idols to Elvis, spoke honestly and unrelentingly of all social matters, and the music was backed up by unstoppable locomotive rhythms. Elvis' conversion to rhythm and blues was total, carving out a path that all American teenagers would soon take.

Carl Perkins, author and original performer of "Blue Suede Shoes," began playing guitar at the age of three.

The rockabilly sound was not solely, as some have described, a cashing-in on the rock craze. On the contrary, it was an exciting hybrid of the homespun expression of country and the driving rhythms of rock and roll. After all, the children brought up on country music heard the same songs on the radio and saw the same images through the wonder of television as did the next American child.

One would be hard put to call Elvis an impersonator of other idioms; rather, he was the genuine product of a growing multicultural experience. Carl Perkins (1932–), the author of "Blue Suede Shoes," the Everly Brothers, Brenda Lee, and Wanda Jackson redefined the parameters of country music to include the fact of an increasingly diverse American culture.

Despite the successes of a few female performers, women were not yet accepted into the music business. Although rockabilly heralded the beginning of an end to the preconceived notions of women's roles and responsibilities, the Puritan ethic remained strong. Television and film could not show men and women, even married, sleeping in bed together. At this time, women and history were still only awkwardly courting.

On top of his success as a guitarist and performer, Chet Atkins was also a talent scout, a producer, and the vice president of RCA Records.

The Nashville Sound

Teenagers interested in the ever-changing American sound began buying records at a staggering pace during the late fifties. As country music expanded commercially into the financially growing world of popular music, Nashville became a central location for country stars. Rather than exporting the burgeoning southern music business to

New York (and the northern phonograph industry in general), southern entrepreneurs decided to keep business local, confident that with
the success of the Grand Ole Opry, Nashville's new recording industry would flourish.

Musicians who came to Nashville during this time began
running in a tight circle of consistently employed, gifted musicians.
The new Nashville sound was a product of cool jazz and the

*The Grand Ole Opry's original home was in this building in Nashville,
near Music Row.*

Wanda Jackson (1937–)

Although Wanda Jackson never made the turn into the top ten, she consistently placed in the twenties on the pop and country charts for fifteen years, and her raucous, sexual, rockabilly persona paved the way for future women of rock and roll.

Born in Maud, Oklahoma, October 29, 1937, Wanda began to be interested in music at the age of six, when her father taught her to play the guitar. By the age of nine she was playing piano and at twelve was performing daily fifteen-minute (soon to be half-hour) radio spots at KLPR in Oklahoma City, near her hometown of Maud. She quickly became the most popular radio personality in the region.

Hank Thompson invited her to sing with his band The Brazos Valley Boys in 1954, and together they began to pump out hits like "You Cain't Have My Love," a duet with Billy Gray and Jackson that reached number eight on the country charts. With a contract soon following from Decca Records, Wanda began touring in 1955 as a solo act, opening for Thompson and Elvis.

Wanda recalls that it was Elvis who convinced her to become a rockabilly performer, stating that the country-rock fusion was soon to become the rage (as it did) and she should get on the bandwagon. An evening with Elvis and his collection of black blues records convinced Jackson that rockabilly was for her.

Unfortunately, the world of music in general was not ready for the sexual revolution. Even Elvis, appearing on *The Ed Sullivan Show*, could not be shown from the waist down. A woman with a healthy appetite for life was not about to cross the threshold of liberation just yet. At the Grand Ole Opry, Wanda was asked to cover her bare shoulders. Even noodle straps at this time were considered too sexy for public viewing. Wanda's career suffered not from a lack of interest but from the denial of the spectacle that garnered her attention.

Her success was soon measured outside the United States; she became one of the first country stars to achieve international stardom. With her screeching rendition of "Fujiyama Mama," Wanda became an overnight sensation in Japan; in Germany, with a song called "Santo Domingo," Wanda finally gained the acknowledgment of her astounding ability.

As a songwriter she also found success with Buck Owens' rendition of her "Kicking Our Hearts Around" and with her own recording of "Right or Wrong," which was released in 1961. With her husband Wendell Goodman as manager during the sixties, Jackson became the star of her own television series, *Music Village*.

By the late sixties she had returned to a more conservative country format. In the seventies, finally tired of the limitations put on her by Capitol Records, Jackson returned to the music of her childhood, gospel, recording with MYRRH and World Records. Now with the Swedish label Tab Records, Wanda is able to record all the types of music she likes—without limitations.

The Jordanaires, a barbershop and gospel group founded in 1948, got their big break in 1956, when they took top honors on Arthur Godfrey's Talent Scouts *show.*

elimination, until the late sixties, of the steel guitar and fiddle. The rock influence slowly gave way to a cleaner, more widely acceptable sound.

Guitarist Chet Atkins (1924–), then head of RCA Victor's country music division, led a progressive jazz group that originated "the sound." With pianist Floyd Cramer (whose greatest influence, he states, was the guitar work of Maybelle Carter), bassist Bob Moore, guitarists Hank Garland and Grady Martin, and drummer Buddy Harman, Atkins produced most of the recordings of popular country music in Nashville's early production history.

Two vocal groups, the Jordanaires and the Anita Kerr Singers, had a major impact on studio singing and were essential to the Nashville sound. Being classically trained professionals, these background country vocalists caused the Nashville sound to become an institutionalized craft, complete with ladders to climb and apprenticeships to complete.

Patsy Cline (1932–1963)

She called herself "the Cline." Patsy Cline, a brassy woman, tested the mettle of many performers just to see them squirm. When they did so, she let out a laugh that started at her big toes and wound through the roof. Those who knew her professionally saw in Patsy a self-determined woman with little care in the world for what others thought.

What the listening audience knew of her, however, was that she was a woman who gave away 100 percent of herself every time she performed. The longing and sadness that seemed so obvious in her tones, the growl and cry, the yodel break that accented the most tragic words in a phrase, were buried deep within a hearty, life-loving personality. Until it was time to sing—to face the truth as she knew it—the Cline was as tough as nails.

Although Patsy Cline's recording career was brief, cut short by a tragic plane crash in 1963, her impact on country music continues to this day. Born Virginia Patterson Hensley on September 8, 1932, Patsy began her amateur career as a child, tap dancing and playing piano. She was a regular performer with her mother at her hometown church in Gore, Virginia.

Her professional debut came as a teenager singing with Bill Peers and the Melody Boys, and at the age of twenty Patsy married her first husband, Gerald Cline, whom she divorced five years later.

Patsy made several trips to Nashville and other big cities, trying to advance her career. She appeared on radio shows such as Roy Acuff's *WSM Dinner Bell*, a conservative family hour, as well as Washington, D.C.'s *Town and Country Time*.

In 1955 she was approached by 4 Star, a California-based record company, to record their songs. Her work for the company, as was standard in those days, was paid for with a flat fee, without royalties. In addition, she did not own the rights to the material she sang and her contract stipulated that she could only perform songs given to her by the company. Although none of her recordings from 4 Star were successful, she was able to promote her voice on vinyl to radio stations; she was lucky enough to get out of her agreement with the recording company before 4 Star was shut down by the IRS.

Quonset Studios, a Nashville-based recording company, was breaking ground with a whole new sound. Traditional accompaniments were being revised to suit the needs of the popular market. Owen Bradley, producer of Patsy Cline's greatest hits, was at the forefront of the Nashville sound. The steel guitar and fiddle were becoming old hat to the movers and shakers of Nashville, so newer, cleaner elements, such as trained background vocalists and classical string instrumentation, were grafted onto country music for the first time. To Patsy, this sound was foreign and had very little to do with the music she so loved. Hesitantly, she began recording her greatest hits.

An appearance on Arthur Godfrey's *Talent Scouts* rocketed her song "Walking After Midnight" to number three on *Billboard's* country chart, and, as Owen Bradley had suspected it might, to the pop charts, at number seventeen.

From that moment on, Cline pumped out (with the help of Bradley and Decca Records) one hit after another. "I Fall to Pieces" and "Crazy" have become country classics. In 1960 she began as a regular performer on the Grand Ole Opry, helping promote her image and opus. The year 1962 proved a sensational one for Patsy Cline, with hits like "She's Got You" and "When I Get Through to You (You'll Love Me Too)" placing high on the charts. On

*Patsy Cline, the first female country singer to appear at the
Hollywood Bowl and Carnegie Hall, was forced to quit school
at the age of fifteen, when her father abandoned the family.*

March 3, 1963, Patsy and two other country music legends, Lloyd Cowboy Copas (author of "Signed, Sealed, Delivered") and Hawkshaw Hawkins (husband of Jean Shepard), were killed in a plane crash caused by bad weather near Camden, Tennessee, on their way back to Nashville from a Kansas City benefit. At thirty-one, Patsy Cline had been singing her songs to audiences for over twenty years.

Her final hit, "Sweet Dreams," was recorded just before her death and released posthumously, also scoring big on both the country and pop charts.

Louisiana's honky-tonk star Faron Young, one of Patsy Cline's former lovers, has had his tunes kept alive by such present-day performers as Reba McEntire.

The list of successful Nashville Sound solo singers comprised a handful of gifted musicians who were brought into the craze and treated as royalty. Patti Page ("Tennessee Waltz"), Patsy Cline (singer of Willie Nelson's "Crazy"), Marty Robbins ("At the End of a Long and Lonely Day"), Ferlin Huskey ("Wings of a Dove"), Don Gibson ("I Can't Stop Loving You"), and Faron Young ("Hello Walls") pumped out hit after hit during this period.

Even today performers who made their names during the Nashville Sound era, such as Patsy Cline, are still marketable country stars (the 1990 re-release of Cline's greatest hits has sold more than three million copies to date).

Folk Movement

In the midst of a century defined by constant change came a revival in traditional American music that furthered the advances of women in country music. Through the reevaluation of the songs and struggles of women from earlier in the twentieth century, the women of the sixties acknowledged the foundations for equality that had been laid by the likes of Maybelle Carter and began the final push toward self-determined careers. A new and courageous sisterhood born from this reevaluation brought to country music, in the sixties and in following decades, a new type of heroine embodying the ideals of liberation.

Boots Randolph, Johnny Cash, and Opry star George Hamilton IV are among the country entertainers who have recorded and performed songs written by Joni Mitchell (above).

Four women brought the history of country music full circle: the Carter Family, this time with the two daughters of the original family, made the Carter mark on country music all over again. With Mama Maybelle at the helm and with the help of June's new love, Johnny Cash, the family quickly regained the

Emmylou Harris (1947–)

With a beautiful, truly southern voice, Emmylou Harris has carved out an eclectic career in both country and urban folk music. By the time Emmylou found her way to the folk scene in Greenwich Village, New York City, in the mid-seventies, it was quickly fading. Although she was able to record an album for Jubilee Records in 1969 called *Gliding Bird*, she soon realized she would have to move or face leaving the music business altogether. Moving to Washington, D.C., she began working at the Cellar Door Club, where she met singer-songwriter Gramm Parsons. From 1971 until Parson's death in 1973, Emmylou recorded and toured with him. Their last album together, *Grievous Angel*, was critically acclaimed.

From cheerleader to valedictorian to beauty queen, country star Emmylou Harris has been a success since childhood.

Reprise Records offered Harris a recording contract in 1974 and the following year she released *Pieces of the Sky*, a rock and country album that did not bring her much exposure. One song from the album was recorded later by the Louvin Brothers, "If I Could Only Win Your Love," which reached the country top ten.

With the help of Elvis Presley's former band, Harris embarked on a successful European tour that led to the recording of her first Grammy-winning album, *Elite Hotel* (1976), which had two hit singles, "Sweet Dreams" and "One of These Days."

By the late seventies, Emmylou's music was moving closer and closer to standard country and further away from the rock-roots tradition she had begun her career with. Her album *Luxury Liner* (1977) included a hit single written by Jimmy Works, "Making Believe."

She also recorded country standards, such as Loretta Lynn's "Blue Kentucky Girl," which was the title cut on Harris' 1979 album. On her *Quarter Moon in a Ten Cent Town* (1978), she covered Dolly Parton's composition "To Daddy," which shot to number three on the country chart. From 1976 to the present Emmylou Harris has worked with just about everyone in country music, from Buck Owens ("That Lovin' Feelin' Again") to Roy Orbison (1936–1989), Don Williams, Dolly Parton, and Linda Ronstadt (1946–).

spotlight. Their appearances on Cash's television series as well as their appearances with him on the road clinched the new Carter Family's success.

The traditional definition of country music during the sixties was expanding to include folk yet again. Women and their messages in the folk arena were becoming more politically conscious without losing the intimate quality that had made the music so appealing. Musicians like Joan Baez (1941–), Judy Collins (1939–), and Joni Mitchell (1943–) have had a great influence on the music of today's female country performers.

Groups like The Stoneman Family Revival, for instance, an early hillbilly band kept alive by the children of the original group, saw a reawakening of interest in their work some thirty years after their original heyday.

Singer-songwriter Joan Baez has made albums in Nashville since 1968. Her first album recorded in Music City, One Day at a Time, *sold more than a million copies.*

While men in country music continued during this period to sing about their right to be rowdy and their general indifference to interpersonal relations (with performers like George Jones at the helm), the female country star spoke from the heart. This era was the beginning of the end of a male-dominated country music industry. The assumptions continually made concerning the "ideal country image" began falling apart. Yet even as the messages of female country performers grew and changed healthily, the lyrics of their male counterparts continued to reflect the traditional (i.e., outdated) roles of men and women.

Success

As had happened during World War II, a glut of talented female musicians became successful during the years of the Vietnam War. This time, unlike the years following World War II, the women were not going away once the boys returned home. For the first time in history, women were going to share in the navigation of country music.

Mary Ann Ward, otherwise known as Marion Worth, became an overnight success with "Shake Me I Rattle (Squeeze Me I Cry)" in 1963.

Loretta Lynn (1935–)

Just when country music seemed through with telling the rural American story, Loretta Lynn, "The Coal Miner's Daughter," put the "country" back into the ever-changing definition of popular southern music.

Born in Butcher Hollow, Kentucky (a town so small that its location is described in relation to another small town, Van Lear), Loretta lived the life expected of an impoverished Kentucky female, marrying her husband, Oliver V. "Mooney" Lynn, at the age of thirteen. Moving her new family to Bellingham, Washington, Loretta began her career as a singer in honky tonks and on the radio.

Loretta Lynn's songs have always caused controversy. "Adam's Rib (To Women's Lib)," "Rated X," and her smash hit "The Pill" are credited with bringing the feminist perspective to country music.

At twenty-five she cut her first single, "Honky Tonk Girl," which she ambitiously marketed to every radio station and music industry agent in her surrounding area. She was picked up the following year by the Wilburn Brothers' talent agency, which immediately had her signed to Decca Records.

Thus began a series of television performances that exposed her to the general public for the first time. Appearances on the Wilburn Brothers' own syndicated television show as well as an appearance on the Grand Ole Opry insured her place in the heart of America.

It is Lynn's lyrics that have guaranteed her place as the sixties' Queen of Country Music. Her honest, thought-provoking words consistently cut to the heart of the subject at hand. Her hits from the sixties, which include "Don't Come Home A' Drinkin' (With Lovin' on Your Mind)" and "Fist City," provide a woman's perspective on a male-dominated world.

With the help of her autobiography, *Coal Miner's Daughter*, written in 1970 (and made into a movie of the same name in 1980, starring Sissy Spacek as Lynn), Loretta Lynn became a legend in her own lifetime.

Dottie West (1932–1983)

Dottie West was another country star raised in abject poverty. The oldest of ten children, Dottie worked to put food on the table—her father deserted the family when she was still a teenager.

By many country music historians' accounts, Dottie West may well have been the first truly liberated woman of country. At first conforming to the accepted roles of women, West did an about-face nearly halfway through her career. Her music, lyrics, and persona changed from the image of the happy housewife to the picture of a woman who desires and demands more from life.

Dorothy Marsh (Dottie's given name) grew up in a family of ten children who, by the time Dottie was fourteen, had been abandoned by their father. The majority of her and her siblings' time was spent helping their mother run a small neighborhood restaurant near their home. Upon graduating from high school, the young and beautiful Dorothy made her way to Tennessee Tech, following her dreams of becoming a musician. While studying there she met her first husband, Bill West, a steel guitar player. Both would soon become professional musicians in Nashville. Once in Nashville, the couple quickly became close friends with other aspiring songwriters. Willie Nelson, Roger Miller (1936–1992), and Dottie West, all at that time unsuccessful, were to be friends for the rest of her life.

The Wests had four children together, three of whom were boys—Morris, Kerry, and Dale. Their only daughter, Shelly West, has become a country star like her mother. The Wests' marriage failed after twenty years, leaving Dottie free to navigate an entirely new path for herself both professionally and personally.

Before their divorce Dottie's self-image was based on her role as mother and wife. The songs she sang were carefully chosen so as not to give any other impression. At one time, in fact, she refused to sing a

Kris Kristofferson song because the lyrics were too sexy. Directly following the divorce, however, she recorded the racy "She Can't Get My Love Off the Bed." Something had definitely changed for West.

Although she had always been described as a positive thinker, happiness for Dottie was fleeting. It was as if, when joy was found, the euphoria of love and good luck would quickly disappear into the mundane routine of daily living. Her need for companionship led her to marry her drummer, twenty-nine-year-old Byron Metcalf, a man fifteen years her junior. Within only a couple of years, however, the happiness had disappeared without notice again, leading to their sudden separation and divorce.

As if West's marriage to a man fifteen years younger wasn't enough to set Nashville on its ear, rumors began spreading after the second divorce that she was keeping a veritable stable of young men, mainly new country talent. In fact, Larry Gatlin (1948–) was "discovered" by Dottie (apparently while Gatlin was living at West's mansion).

At the age of fifty, Dottie West again remarried, this time to Alan Winters, age twenty-eight, who was West's sound engineer. Following their marriage, Alan, a farm boy from Pennsylvania, left the road to watch over Dottie's fifty-acre ranch and to tend their gorgeous garden. With experience under her belt from two other marriages, Dottie thought it wise that the two of them not be on the road together.

Even caution, however, could not keep the sun from setting on Dottie West's happiness.

Seven years after their marriage, in 1983, the two were divorced. The ranch Alan had tended was soon foreclosed and their valuables sold off to pay over two and a half million dollars in debts, the majority of which was owed to the IRS. On top of all this, Dottie had two car crashes within that same year. The first hospitalized her and the second killed her. On her way to the Grand Ole Opry, the car she was being driven in (she no longer owned a car) careened off the ramp on Nashville's parkway. After three operations to remove damaged organs, West's heart gave out.

The world will always remember Dottie West. "Here Comes My Baby," her Grammy-winning single, "Every Time Two Fools Collide," and "What Are We Doing in Love?" are not just songs but permanent memories of Dottie West.

Songwriter and performer Willie Nelson was a good friend of Dottie West, and like her suffered at the hands of the IRS.

Melba Montgomery's hit song about a mother's love, "No Charge," went to number one on Mother's Day in 1974.

Some of the most recognizable talents to arrive on the scene during this period were Skeeter Davis, Loretta Lynn, Marion Worth, Tammy Wynette, Jan Howard (1932–), Jean Shepard (1933–), Dolly Parton, Norma Jean (1938–), Jeannie Seely (1940–), Dottie West, Connie Smith (1941–), and Melba Montgomery (1938–). Now, some thirty years later, we know who of that list ended up taking the reins. At the time of their arrivals, however, each performer, through sheer talent, honesty, and tenacity, put herself in the running to become the next Queen of Country.

Melba Montgomery, for instance, had a meteoric rise to fame in 1963. Determined to perform the music as purely as possible, as many folk artists were doing at this same time, Melba relied on acoustic instrumentation, including the use of the Dobro, and simple recording techniques. Her most memorable songs came from

Tammy Wynette (1942–)

"The Heroine of Heartbreak" was born Virginia Wynette Pugh on May 15, 1942, on her grandfather's cotton farm in Itawamba County, Mississippi. Upon the death of her father, a cotton farmer, Tammy's mother went to work in a Birmingham defense plant during World War II, leaving the eight-month-old girl to be raised by her grandparents.

Married for the first time at the age of seventeen, Wynette was soon the mother of three, the youngest of whom never fully recovered from spinal meningitis. Working as a hairdresser, she carefully managed their meager income to pay for food, rent, and the sick child's medical expenses.

After several unsuccessful trips to Nashville to break into the business, and a divorce from her first husband, Virginia Pugh finally had a bit of good luck with an introduction to Billy Sherrill (1936–). Having an ear for a good song and a knack for image making, Sherrill soon changed Virginia's name and found her her first hit. "Apartment #9" was the beginning of a career that has now shone for over twenty-five years. In 1967 and 1968, both very big years for Wynette, she hit the charts with "Your Good Girl's Gonna Go Bad," "D-I-V-O-R-C-E," and the immortal "Stand By Your Man."

Her success, as well as more personal troubles, continued with her marriage to legendary singer and drinker George Jones. Not surprisingly, this turmoil led to many more country hits for Wynette, with duets like "Did You Ever," "Two Story House," and "Southern California," which were written by friend Billy Sherrill and future husband George Richey.

Tammy Wynette, now the mother of six children, has survived five marriages, several hospitalizations for depression, and, of all strange things, a kidnapping. Surprisingly, Tammy has stayed as youthfully beautiful and engagingly honest an artist as she was the first day America was introduced to her. Wynette is determined to have another twenty-five years of success in country music.

Tammy Wynette has had over seventy hit songs. "Stand by Your Man" is still the best-selling single in the history of women in country music.

Skeeter Davis (1931–   )

Skeeter Davis, born Mary Frances Penick, is the most popular country singer worldwide. Her success in Japan and Europe is astounding, putting her above the likes of Dolly Parton in name recognition.

Her recording career began in 1953, when she performed as part of a duo called The Davis Sisters, which was formed with her best friend from high school, Betty Jack Davis. Their "I Forgot More Than You'll Ever Know" became one of the most popular songs of 1953.

An auto accident ended the life of friend Betty Jack Davis in 1953 and affected Skeeter so deeply that she retired, only to resurface in the late fifties and rise in popularity through the sixties with such favorites as "Set Him Free" and "Optimistic."

best-selling duets with George Jones. "Let's Invite Them Over" and "We Must Have Been Out of Our Minds" are examples of quality songwriting (with strikingly honest lyrics) and down-home southern singing.

The following year Connie Smith became a contender for the title of Queen of Country Music with "Once a Day," by Bill Anderson. The song went straight to number one upon its release.

One of the sure leaders of the pack at the time was Mary Frances Penick, better known as Skeeter Davis. Early in her career in music, some ten years before her rise to fame as a solo star, she was a member of The Davis Sisters. Between the end of her duet career, brought on by the death of her partner Betty Jack Davis, and the beginning of her solo career was a brief retirement. In 1958, however, she began recording again, hitting the charts with "Set Him Free" and "Optimistic." Most who enter the world of country music today will not see the impact that Skeeter has had on the music, as her career has taken on more international than national importance. She is today the most widely successful country music performer in the world (and the most recognized country star in Europe and Japan).

Tammy Wynette and Loretta Lynn both came to the scene with their hearts on their sleeves. "The Heroine of Heart-break" (Wynette) and "The Coal Miner's Daughter" (Lynn) had in common an affinity for the quickly evaporating rural America. These talented women, in distinctively different voices, broke the bad news of the decline of family values in hard times.

Dolly Parton, one decade at a time, became the most popular and, needless to say, richest female country performer in the United States. Today Dolly Parton

Connie Smith (above), Dolly Parton suggests, is one of only "three real women singers" in the United States. "The rest of us are just fakin' it."

owns the largest of all the self-constructed shrines in country music, Dollywood, an amusement park with herself as the main theme, that is proof of her popularity as an entertainer and the power she wields as a businesswoman.

Dolly Parton (1946–)

Native Tennessean Dolly Parton is estimated to be worth seventy million dollars and is one of the five most powerful women in show business. With the voice of an angel, the brains of a great businesswoman, and undeniably good looks, Parton has done more with a high school education than almost any other person in the world. From abject poverty on Locust Ridge to her legendary status in Nashville, Parton has carved out a brilliant path for herself.

The first member of her family to graduate from high school, Dolly Parton is today one of the most successful women in the entertainment industry.

Being the granddaughter of a minister meant an early introduction to the traditional church music that is the backbone of country. Her talents were apparent at a very early age. When she was a child, her Knoxville uncles presented her to Tennesseans for the first time on their television program, *Farm and Home*. Parton knew from that moment on she was meant for the spotlight.

Immediately after high school, Dolly Parton moved from her family's shack to Nashville. In her first week in Nashville she met her soon-to-be husband Carl I. Dean. Dean happened to be driving past the Wishy Washy Laundromat in downtown Nashville as Dolly stepped out of the laundromat for a soda. Being from the country, she waved innocently (she admits now that she was flirting, "but only a little") at the tall, dark young man, who immediately circled back to speak with her. Described by those who know him personally as kind and honest, Carl has been given a hard time by the press for almost the entirety of Dolly's career due to his determination to stay out of the limelight. With respect for each other, they have honored each other's needs—Carl remained a private citizen while Dolly conquered the world.

By twenty-one she had appeared regularly on Porter Wagoner's television series, and in the following year, 1968, she began recording with Monument Records. As a songwriter Dolly has had her greatest successes with "Jolene" in 1973, "Coat of Many Colors" in 1971, and "9 to 5."

Whether singing spirituals, mountain ballads, or rock-influenced pop, Dolly brings her considerable musical talents to bear, making each song her own.

The Seventies and Eighties

The 1970s was the era of the "urban cowboy," when the boy was taken out of the country and put into industrialized urban centers (without taking the country out of the boy). During this period, women were consistently portrayed in movies as playing second fiddle to their screen spouses and lovers. What headway was not made by the motion picture industry, however, was being made up for by the women in the commercial music industry.

Now headlining on tours, women began reinforcing their gains in the industry. From the all-important maneuverings for power (women were finally being put in charge of production) to seemingly minor yet significant accomplishments (Jeannie Seely demanded that the Grand Ole Opry stop introducing women as "pretty little gals"), women were demanding more respect and control.

Singer Jeannie Seely is notorious in Nashville for dry, witty lyrics, such as the classic "An ex-husband is one mistake you don't have to live with."

Before she became famous, Canadian country singer Anne Murray was a gym teacher on Prince Edward Island.

As had happened sporadically throughout the twentieth century, country began to appeal to a larger audience in the seventies. The return to popular music formats, as witnessed by the work of performers like Kenny Rogers, Marie Osmond, Anne Murray, and the indestructible Dolly Parton, was a bumpy ride that again favored the fanciful, celluloid image of country musicians. Frilly cowboy outfits, a mixture of disco-influenced polyester and the singing-cowboy image, brought sales up but the respectability of the music down. Infighting over the direction of country was understandably furious. This conflict was settled only over time, aided by the advent of new, innovative talents.

Remaining true to the roots of the music while still enjoying commercial success during this period were such performers as Jeanne

Singer-songwriter Jeanne Pruett has had her songs covered by such performers as Conway Twitty and Tammy Wynette.

Barbara Mandrell (1948–   )

In Nashville, the largest and most technologically advanced museum built in honor of a country music star stands in honor of Barbara Mandrell. Like all shrines in the Tennessee town, it was built not by adoring fans hoping to crown her queen, but rather by the idol herself.

"Since I'm a fan of yours, please sign the registry at the front door." Barbara smiles widely from the TV screen above the adoring crowd, "Welcome to Barbara Mandrell Country." She waves her hand in the direction of the next entranceway, signaling the crowd to the next room of the sanctuary.

The shrine wasn't built in a day. In fact, the long journey to becoming a Nashville legacy started early in childhood. When she was only eleven years old, Barbara already played the banjo, steel guitar, and saxophone. Her father, Irby Mandrell, to this day still proudly states that his daughter could read sharps and flats before she could read words.

During her teenage years Barbara, then called "The Sweetheart of the Steel Guitar," played with her family band. Father Irby was on guitar, sister Louise sang, and Barbara's future husband, Ken Dudney, played drums. Raised to believe that women shouldn't leave their parents' house until they are married, Barbara got hitched as soon as she turned eighteen and left the family band forever.

A year out of the music business was enough time for her to reassess her life ambitions. Visiting the Grand Ole Opry with her father, Barbara finally confided in him that she felt she was on the wrong side of the microphone. (Her father agreed, and to this day manages Barbara's career.)

Three hundred engagements a year meant nearly every day was spent on the road. Already a mother, Barbara decided to bring her family on tour with her. In fact, her son Matthew lived on the road for the majority of his childhood. In Matthew's eyes, the decision to bring him along was the smartest choice. To this day he remembers the circuit fondly, especially the days spent at county and state fairs. Her daughter, Jaime, has spent less time on tour than her older brother, thanks to the fame that finally caught up with Barbara. The youngest of the Mandrell family, Nathaniel, isn't likely ever to spend consecutive days on the road.

The Barbara Mandrell television show gave Barbara the chance to prove to the United States her worthiness as a musician to those in and outside country music, establishing her among the nation's most recognizable talents.

Since Barbara's infamous car accident in 1984 (from which she took nearly two years to recover) she has had more time for her family. She has expanded her goals to include more television production and building a dreamhouse for her family.

Jeannie C. Riley's hit, "Harper Valley PTA," hit number one on the pop charts, earned a Grammy, won country's 1968 Single of the Year, and sold more than five million copies.

Pruett (1937–), the singer of "Satin Pillows," Jeannie C. Riley (1945–), who sang "Harper Valley PTA," and Donna Fargo (1949–), who sang "The Happiest Girl in the Whole USA." Tanya Tucker (1958–), at the age of sixteen, became an overnight sensation with the hit "Delta Dawn." Down to her age, size, and firecracker personality, Tanya had a striking resemblance to the rockabilly heroine Brenda Lee.

The Judds, Naomi (left) and Wynonna (formerly Diana and Christina, respectively), have sold more than ten million albums and won more than fifty entertainment awards.

The "wild child" of country, Tanya Tucker has made her own choices professionally and personally. Her fans are not alone in admiring her; in 1991, she was honored with an award from the Country Music Association.

The 1980s brought to the stage three very successful women. Two of them, the Judds, were a mother/daughter duet who for ten years produced hit after hit. Naomi (1946–) and Wynonna (1964–) have since, due to Naomi's failing health, stopped performing as a team, but Wynonna, now a star in her own right, carries on the family's reputation and music.

Originally "The Sweetheart of the Steel Guitar" while in her family band as a teenager, Barbara Mandrell became the most popular female singer of the eighties, winning two Entertainer of the Year awards. Barbara is very much a unique phenomenon: she has an astounding instrumental talent (she plays five instruments), a beautiful singing voice, and an amazing business sense.

Today and Tomorrow

Today the women of country are speaking for themselves and reaping the rewards of their honesty and perseverance. Although the battle is by no means over, barrier-breaking women like Mary-Chapin Carpenter, educated at Brown University, k.d. lang (1962–), a Canadian singer with a powerful voice and an unconventional

Unafraid of controversy, one of country music's most outspoken stars, k.d. lang, promoted vegetarianism in an ad campaign labeled "Meat Stinks," despite angry reactions from many sides.

image, and Rosanne Cash, whose deeply felt songs reveal a prodigious talent all her own, make up a new breed of female performers who represent a profound change in country music.

Performers like Pam Tillis (1957–), daughter of Mel Tillis, Reba McEntire (1954–), Suzi Boggus (1956–), Ronna Reeves, Trisha Yearwood (1964–), Kathy Mattea (1959–), Michele Wright (1961–), Becky Hobbs (1950–), and Lorrie Morgan (1959–) carry on the traditions of honky tonk, the Nashville sound, and country swing while speaking from the heart about the real lives of women—and men—

Rosanne Cash (1955–)

Being the heiress to the throne of country music is not necessarily a blessing. In fact, in the case of Rosanne Cash, the inheritance led to an unsettled life, where recovering from near-death experiences, for instance, is more commonplace than one might think.

What Rosanne perceived as the common experience during her childhood would be considered tragic by most other people's standards. Only a toddler when her father, Johnny Cash, became a world-renowned country singer, Rosanne and her family lived in daily anxiety and confusion. Only months before Rosanne could walk, Johnny was simply an appliance salesman, the first generation of his family to work outside of sharecropping. This workingman's strapping son had a talent that would quickly push him beyond the world he understood. As Rosanne puts it, "Nobody's prepared for that kind of fame"—not the one who gains the fame nor the family he or she brings into it.

Rosanne's approach toward life—however hesitant she may be to admit it—was and is much like her father's. When things became too stable in their lives the music in their minds began to stagnate. Recognition of this waning inspiration often led to drastic reactions. Father and daughter have both questioned the calm they have achieved for themselves, and in examining that feeling of stability, have taken steps to abolish it.

After the divorce of Rosanne's parents, the four Cash daughters went to live with their mother and her new husband, a police officer in Ventura, California. As children often do in dysfunctional families, Rosanne, Cindy, Kathy, and Tara began acting out against every institution around them. Rosanne, in particular, was real trouble for her teachers in high school. At times she would drop her younger siblings off at school, pick up her boyfriend, and head for Tijuana. Trouble was a balm to the fury she had inherited.

Rosanne spent a year in London after high school and then attended Vanderbilt University for a while, until she moved to Los Angeles to study acting. Finally coming to terms with the fact that her talent—songwriting and singing—meant competing with her father and in a sense recognizing his influence on her, Rosanne moved to Nashville and began putting together a set with her future husband Rodney Crowell, a gifted songwriter and guitarist who had made his name with Emmylou Harris. Rosanne Cash's first album, *Right or Wrong*, was a combined effort by Crowell and Cash.

As her father had after his first big success, Rosanne developed a healthy drug addiction following the release of her album *Seven Year Ache*, in 1981. Rosanne, now out of control, was hospitalized by her family (as Johnny had been by his family years before) in the hopes of restoring the daughter (and wife) sadly displaced by fame. (She has since fully recovered.)

In 1985 she released *Rhythm and Romance*, which won her a Grammy that year for best country vocal performance by a female. *King's Record Shop*, a collection of songs that were for the most part made famous by other artists, paid homage to the music she loves. From that album came four number one country singles.

Since then Rosanne Cash has crossed over from country to rock and folk at Columbia Records, left her husband Crowell, and moved to New York City, doing what Cashes do best—shaking things up for the sake of a fresh start.

today. K.T. Oslin (1942–), a former television and stage star, took to singing as a career late in life and has in the last five years overcome prejudices concerning both her age and gender. Indeed, many of the performers in country music today are women, and they are commanding higher record and ticket sales than they ever have before.

Mary-Chapin Carpenter's stardom came with her song "Never Had It So Good" from her top-ten album of 1989, State of the Heart.

The current success of country is likely to continue as long as the music speaks to the here and now. As the twentieth century draws to a close, songwriters find themselves saying goodbye and paying homage to the past while trying to make sense of the present. Definitions of male and female roles have been revised continuously over the last half of the twentieth century and each artist has struggled to find personal meaning in an ever-changing world. The women of country have held up a mirror to society, allowing people to see in its reflection the good, the bad, and the ugly aspects of modern life. The hoped-for effect of music is to change things for the better—the hard-won success of women in country music attests to its power. With integrity and courage, these women have carved out a respected (and profitable) place for women in the world of country music.

With Patsy Montana, the first woman to have a record sell a million copies, women gained the right to equal pay—as long as they were playing the cowboy's sweetheart. During

Rosanne Cash's "My Baby Thinks He's a Train" and "Blue Moon with Heartache" both went to number one on the country charts in 1981 with the release of her album Seven Year Ache.

the heyday of honky tonk, Kitty Wells was able to speak out against men who hid behind a double standard —but only from the perspective of the "good woman." In the sixties, Loretta Lynn and Tammy Wynette demanded the right to speak the hard truth—but found little opportunity to change the order of things.

The women of country music today are of a new generation, for whom the limitations of the past no longer exist. Country performers in general are responding to the demands of a new audience. Today's country fans are found all over the map and at every level of society, young and old, male and female, rich and poor.

In the United States, country music at present makes up 55 percent of the entire music industry. All other forms of

Mary-Chapin Carpenter (1958–)

What is the role of country music in a society that left the agrarian age more than one hundred years ago? Where are we headed, economically and personally, today? Mary-Chapin Carpenter captures the essence of our time and place today through lyrics about ghost towns and gone-but-not-forgotten loves. In a society riddled with divorce and disenfranchisement, her music pays homage to the past, without resentment or indictment. Her music bears all the signs of a changing society, redefining the role of country music by speaking to the needs of women and men today.

Mary-Chapin, whose music reveals a strong connection to "average" people, was not raised in an average family. Her mother, Bowie, worked at a private school while raising Mary-Chapin and her three sisters. Her father, Chapin, was an executive at *Life* magazine. These extraordinarily intelligent people were able to balance the comparitively luxurious life they led with the realities of the rest of the world, keeping Mary-Chapin and her siblings in touch with the struggles of the less fortunate. Through travel and a strong education the Carpenter children gained a compassionate and informed view of the world.

In 1969 Chapin Carpenter was assigned to the Asian edition of *Life,* so the family left their home in Princeton, New Jersey, and moved to Japan. After two years abroad, Mary-Chapin and her family resettled in Washington, D.C. Back in the United States, Mary-Chapin attended Taft Prep School in Connecticut. After graduation from Taft, she attended Brown University, where she received a Bachelor of Arts in American Civilization.

By 1983 she had moved back to Washington, D.C., trying her hand at live performance while working during the day as an administrative assistant with a Washington-based philanthropic group. Carpenter's first few years back in D.C. were spent getting over shyness and general stage fright while friends and colleagues ambitiously promoted her songs to local radio stations.

Finally, in 1987, she signed with CBS Records and recorded her debut album, *Hometown Girl*, with friend and coproducer John Jennings in Jennings' basement. Although Mary-Chapin was now signed with a major label, the next two years were still profitless. She held on to her day job while touring when possible, always lugging equipment around in her car.

The star treatment from CBS Records did not begin until 1990, when she received a standing ovation at the 1990 CMA awards ceremony for her performance of "You Don't Know Me (I'm the Opening Act)." With this honor also came a bus and crew to move all the equipment around for her and the members of the band.

She finally hit the top in 1991 with the release of her single "Down at the Twist and Shout," which deservedly brought her the prized Grammy award for best country vocal performance by a female. Her fourth album, *Come On Come On*, went platinum; songs like "I Feel Lucky" and "He Thinks He'll Keep Her" have made Mary-Chapin Carpenter and her music an institution.

A folk musician by nature, Carpenter has brought country music full circle. The term "country" has been used for the last eighty years to point out the differences between city and rural folk. Now that folk music is again being accepted into the realm of country, the audience for country music is defying regional and educational boundaries.

popular music combined do not have the influence that country has. What was once believed to be a low-brow form is now a power-broker's business. At the same time, country owes its success to the abilities of performers to touch the hearts of listeners.

Country music has always tackled the topics of profoundest concern to women and men alike—the joy and pain of love and heartbreak, the struggle to make a living in an uncaring world, the consequences of doing right and wrong. The women of country have carried on this tradition with great courage and style, enriching and expanding it by making country music meaningful to a whole new generation of listeners. Building on the legacy of talent and toughness handed down by pioneering female performers, the women of country are clearly here to stay.

After spending a dozen years avoiding country music, Pam Tillis climbed quickly up the country charts with the release of "Don't Tell Me What to Do" in 1991.

Bibliography

Carlyle, Dolly. "How D. West Was Won." *People*, September 12, 1983.

Corliss, Richard. "Come On, Come On." *Time*, August 24, 1992.

Cornfield, Robert, with Marshall Fallwell, Jr. *Just Country: Country People, Stories and Music*. New York: McGraw-Hill, 1976.

Dellar, Fred. *The Illustrated Encyclopedia of Country Music*. New York: Harmony Books, 1977.

Dougherty, Steve, and Margie Sellinger. "Urbane Cowgirl Blues." *People*, September 30, 1992.

Gates, David. "Nashville's Shrines: Memories, Stars and Famous Guitars." *Smithsonian*, March 1988.

Grissim, John. *Country Music: White Man's Blues*. Philadelphia: Coronet Books, 1970.

Kaylin, Lucy. "She Walks the Line." *GQ*, September 1991.

Lynn, Loretta. *Coal Miner's Daughter*. Chicago: H. Ragnery, 1976.

Morris, Edward. "Barbara Mandrell and Family." *McCall's*, May 1988.

Nash, Alanna. *Dolly*. Los Angeles: Reed Books, 1978.

Sadie, Stanley. *New Grove Dictionary of American Music*. Washington, D.C.: Macmillan Publishing, 1980.

Sandberg, Larry, and Dick Weissman. *The Folk Music Sourcebook*. New York: Da Capo, 1989.

Sanz, Cynthia, and Jane Sanderson. "Goodbye Sunshine." *People*, September 16, 1991.

"Sharps, Flats at Age 5." *U.S. News and World Report*, June 20, 1983.

Suggested Reading

Bekker, Peter O.E. *Country*. New York: Friedman/Fairfax Publishers, 1993.

Carter, Jeanette. *Living with Memories*. Hiltons, Va.: Carter Family Memorial Music Center, 1983.

Jones, Jacqueline. *The Dispossessed*. New York: BasicBooks, 1992.

Malone, Bill C. *Country Music USA*. Austin, Tex.: University of Texas Press, 1968.

Nash, Alanna. *Behind Closed Doors: Talking with the Legends of Country*. New York: Knopf, 1988.

Wynette, Tammy, with Joan Dew. *Stand By Your Man*. New York: Simon and Schuster, 1979.

Suggested Listening

Carpenter, Mary-Chapin. *Come On Come On*. Columbia.

The Carter Family. *Clinch Mountain Treasures*. County.

Cash, Rosanne. *King's Record Shop*. CBS.

Cline, Patsy. *The Last Sessions*. Decca.

Davis, Skeeter. *Skeeter Davis and NRBQ: She Sings, They Play*. Rounder.

Harris, Emmylou. *Blue Kentucky Girl*. Warner Brothers.

Jackson, Wanda. *Rockin' in the Country*. RHINO Records.

Lee, Brenda. *Country Girl*. RCA.

Lynn, Loretta. *Coal Miner's Daughter*. MCA.

Mandrell, Barbara. *Greatest Hits*. MCA.

Parton, Dolly. *Eagle When She Flies*. Columbia.

Wells, Kitty. *Greatest Hits, Vol. I and II*. Step One Records.

Wynette, Tammy. *Anniversary: 20 Years of Hits*. CBS.

Index

Photography Credits